Life in a Dream

Daniel Blair
Wasilla, Alaska USA

ISBN   978-0-615-42323-4
ISBN   10 061542323X
LCCN   2010917998

Printed in the United States of America.

Preface

This book is a heartfelt collection of poems written over time and based on the personal experiences of the author. First in a series, this volume is the hope of the author that his works will touch the reader and lead them into his real life. Daniel Blair writes about life; his own and the lives of those that have touched his life. Join him as he reminisces about his world and be touched as he shares his Life in a Dream with you.

Acknowledgements

I want to thank all my family and friends who supported me in my writing endeavors. It is my hope that they will find themselves in the essence of this book.

My warmest thanks go out to Shirley Harmon who truly knows the importance of how much a teacher can change the life of a student.

Special thanks to Darcy Logan who encouraged me at my lowest point to try to stay focused on pursuing writing.

Table of Contents

CHAPTER TITLE

QUESTIONS

With age comes wisdom so often were told

But through youth and adventure we forge ahead
bold

To seek love and comfort is the one joy we seek

Searching for answers until we are weak

We look back at our lives and the things that we
shared

With special people, we thought would always be
there

Love tossed away in the dead of the night

Where dreams were broken when things didn't
seem right

Where did we go in the lives that we led?

How did we end up alone in our beds?

For days and years have passed so fast it seems

Were we really alive or just part of a dream?

Where did our visions of a perfect life go?

Why did we drift so far from the things that we know?

In our infinite wisdom as we filled out our days

What were our goals as we went on our ways?

Did we dream of a life with no trouble or strife?

Of a perfect world with a husband or wife

Did we dream of a job where success would ring true?

Did we succeed in the things that we struggled to do?

Did we enjoy life to its fullest extent?

Making the most of each day that we spent

Did we stress over things that at the time seemed so tall

When in reality they were tiny and small

Searching our lives as if on a great treasure chase

Living our lives in a great frantic pace

Reaching for dreams that were just out of reach

Did we show this to our children in the words that we preached?

Did we show them the value of chasing your
dreams?
Or wasting your life on bad choices it seems
Where do we go at the end of our days?
Will it be in heaven or burn in hell in some way?
No one knows the answers of the true meaning of
life
So often we are lost in this world full of strife
Did that dent on your car really mean so much in
its time?
Or was it just a bump that turned out just fine
We stressed and worried for most of our days
Living our life in all sorts of ways
Does it seem the harder we try the more things we
regret
How many things would we choose to forget?
All we can do as we pass through our days
Is put trust in God to guide us in some way
So often we are judged by people who don't know
you exist

They don't even know you but still can't resist
To throw stones at a house that is made full of
glass
Blaming you for mistakes that you've made in
your past
All we can do is to try to survive
And enjoy the rest of our days and be truly alive
For the past is the past and can't be undone
What we will really gain in this race that we've run
Today as you look at the days of your past
Try to forget them and the shadows they cast
For tomorrow is brighter with the oncoming sun
Hope for the future with a true special one
Shadows that toil over your soul
Will try to ruin your dreams wherever you go
Reach to the future and to the new day ahead
Never regret the things in your life until you are
dead
Live for your dreams for they are forever with you
Above everything be true to just you.

THE MINER'S WIFE

The life of a miner that lives deep in the hills
Is full of danger that give most men the chills
Where families worry each day above ground
While in the dark hole their loved one is found
The wife of a miner is lonely and cold
But through faith in God she is so often bold
To kiss her dear husband each morning good bye
Not knowing at all if this day he might die
The strength of a woman who must somehow
stand tall
To be the pillar of strength if the mine somehow
falls
To hold together a family with care
To show love for her kinfolk and to always be
there
Fixing breakfast in the early hours of morn
Where feelings of worry in her mind are torn
She looks at the man who is the love of her life

The one she forever will be proud of as his wife
She sees the look on his face as he eats in silence
alone
This gentle man who is solid as stone
Not many words are spoken in the day that's still
dark
As they wait for the whistle of the day shift to start
He knows he must leave to dig deep in the mine
Not knowing at all, what in each day he will find
They sit there in silence with love that is true
Just poor simple people who must do what they do
He provides for his family like his forefathers have
done
This poor simple man, a coal miner's son
She knows the life to well on her own
For in the dark mines her family had grown
Mining the coal so that others can live
Is the one simple gift that they know how to give
He readies himself as he prepares to go
The long lonely drive to the mine to dig coal

For the job is not right down the street
They never know each day if that night they will
meet
She rises on her toes as she kisses his lips
Where three little words "I love you" tenderly slip
Does he see the tear fall gently out of her eye?
As she rearranges her hair so he won't see her cry
For she is a strong woman who knows what she
must do
Be there for him and get their kids off to school
She watches him leave in their old beat up truck
Knowing once in the mine its God's will and good
luck
Her day is filled with worry and stress
Does her family know how well they've been
blessed?
For a miner's wife is hard on the soul
All for the love of a man who digs out the coal
She waits every evening for hours on end

To see the lights of the truck from her lover and
friend
Not many know the lives that they lead
Unless you lived it yourself you don't know of
their deeds
For the miners code will be with you wherever you
go
For all of the people who work deep in earth's soil
Once a miner, you will always be one in your heart
Fearing for others when their world's torn apart
From cave in's to explosions that rip through their
homes
They all come together to leave no one alone
The hills are full of family and friends
Who will always be there through thick or through
thin?
Yes the miner's wife is made of a special mold
The bravest of brave where stories are told
Leaving each day as if it might be the last
Of life as they know it, where God's will is cast

Each night when she sees him arrive with clothes
full of black
Where the eyes of her loved one shines through the
cracks
She never worries at all of the dust on his clothes
She rushes to hug him so he always knows
She loves him so much for day that he gives
So much of his soul, so they somehow can live
Such a simple existence, but yet so much strain
Deep in the hills where their lives will remain
As they drift off to sleep holding each other tight
They whisper "I love you" and know things are all
right.

DEAR KENTUCKY

Sitting here thinking of how life used to be

Remembering days of Dear Kentucky

Closing my eyes the visions are clear

Of life in the hills with the ones I loved dear

Family and friends who were there by my side

Such special gifts that were along for the ride

Days of a youth where memories last

Where life was simple those times from the past

Awakening each day to the smells of the day

Still fill my mind as it drifts far away

The sounds of the rooster echoes deep in my mind

Who needed an alarm clock he always knew the right time

For each day we woke up as he crowed out his song

Wake up sleepy head, the day is half gone

The smell of the dew on the ground early in morn

The glow of the day as the sun kept us warm

Morning Glories vibrant as they opened each day
Their colors glistening as their blooms came out to play
The hills came alive in the early hours of life
Where everyone struggled in their will to survive
Not much has changed in the place we call home
That's one thing we've learned in the miles we've roamed
The people of Kentucky are such a soft hearted breed
Never bragging at all about their lives or their deeds
Where a neighbor is welcome in your home any time
Where a nod of the head or howdy is fine
Sitting for hours on the porch with a friend
Building strong friendships that never would end
Listening to the old men and the stories they tell
Laughing for hours at the lies they told well
Trying to outdo the first lie that was told

Just being among them made you part of the fold
Women who cooked meals fit for a king
The smell from the kitchen was one of my favorite
things
How many nights did we sit on the porch?
Listening to the ball game as if some sort of torch
For life wasn't about TV and the things that we
had
Just plain simple things that made us so glad
Running the mountains in search of some fun
Climbing and running in the days we were young
The sun would break over the hills and turn its
warmth on our day
Begging us children to come out and play
Work in the garden and watch natures surprise
The land would provide right in front of our eyes
Seeing the trucks haul their precious black gold
How many have lived off the land we were told
"Back in my day we didn't have the things that
you do"

Was our constant reminder from the old folks who
knew
"We used to walk to school two miles, uphill both
ways
Yes those were the times son back in my day"
Where school was for learning and not a social
dance
Where girls wore dresses and boys wore nice pants
Funny we think of these things our parents said
How were they so smart to put these things in our
heads?
We've learned many things from the simple people
we knew
Who believed in the Bible and God's love that is
true
He will provide when things don't seem right
That is why we pray, to him on each night
How do you not see the gift of the hills?
When so many of its virtues will give you the
chills

Just sitting at night on the porch as day ends

Surrounded by family, lovers and friends

You can smell the musk of the land as it drifts off to sleep

Smells that will haunt you in the memories you keep

You can smell the rain come before the first lightning strikes

A fragrance so strong as it approaches in flight

You can feel the air change as the storm slowly drifts in

Some memories linger in your mind without end

Watching the rain pour hard to the ground

Would it ever stop, we wondered as it steadily pound

The one thing we knew that at the end of each storm

One of God's gifts, a rainbow would form

We would wait in anticipation for the rainbow to arrive

For at the end of its journey we felt so alive

Seeing the colors break out in the sun

Brought a smile to the face of the old folks and young

Yes the hills of Kentucky have stories and pride

Where friendships are forever and they stand side by side

Home will always be in those hills so true

Where people are friendly and the grass they call blue

I know for myself, in my life I have roamed

But for me Kentucky will forever be home

<u>TEARS</u>

How can the simplest expression that falls from the
eye
Mean so many things, from a simple hello to
death's final good bye
When a tear leaves the eye and falls from the
cheek
Leaving so many defenseless and weak
When the sting of the salt glistens softly off your
face
Crying your tears will never leave you in disgrace
For tears flow from the soul to help ease your heart
When the love of your life seems miles apart
So many tears shed for so many reasons
From the birth of a life to those who commit trea-
son
How many times do we stop deep in thought?
Remembering heroes who gave their life in wars
that were fought

Those who fought and gave the life from their
souls
Not debating at all, as into battle they go
Have you shed a tear for the deeds they have done
Without their sacrifice, would we have won?
The right to be free in this land that we live
Do you stop at all to thank them for the gifts that
they give?
We see the dear children as they say goodbye to
their Dads
Mothers struggling to not show how in their hearts
they were sad
Tears flowing for reasons some of us will not
know
The fear of them dying in wars as they go
The tear of the child as it trembles inside
Where deep in their soul it desperately hides
To not show their parents how much they really
know

Will the tear from their eyes show the depths of
their soul?

Mothers and fathers who go off to war
Are our true heroes as they wade onto shores
The tears that are shed as they go forward to fight
Are shed deep in their blankets on cold lonely
nights
Why are we here? What are we fighting for?
What is the purpose as we struggle for more?
Will we ever see our loved ones alive?
I beg of you Lord to not let me die
For the tears that are shed are never in vain
They are straight from the heart from love and in
pain
To see a fellow soldier die in a land far away
What did the people think of him on his final day?
Were tears shed for the soldier as the life left him
there?
Did anyone know? Did they really care?

To ones left behind to try to fill the void in their place
Crying forever as tears fall from their face
Young men and women die in faraway lands
We ask in our hearts could this be part of God's plan
We fall to our knees as tears stream from our eyes
Why in your wisdom, God did they have to die?
As we remember this day that is etched in our minds
Do we take time in our day to remember that time?
Nine years ago our lives drastically changed
When out of the rubble our souls rearranged
The meaning of tears changed for me forever that day
From the loss of loved ones to the cost that they pay
Yes tears fall for reasons that we will forever see
From the dust of the buildings to the red blood of sea

Cry for the ones left behind of those that were killed
Remember their lives in your heart and your will
As you remember the pictures as their etched in your mind
Shed for these people a tear gentle and kind
Remember our soldiers who fight for our rights
To lay by our loved ones in our homes late at night
For they fight in lands and lay in cold foreign lands
Protecting our rights in their will as they stand
So if you can take a moment in each of your days
To remember these souls as you kneel down to pray
"God give them your love as they fight on this day
Bring them home safely in Your Name we pray"
A tear hits the floor as another soldier lies down to die
Will you remember tomorrow, with a tear from your eye?

DID YOU?

As we travel the roads on our journeys each day
Do we make time in our lives to know God in
some way?
As we hurry and rush in the things that we do
Do we stop and enjoy the things that are true
When we jump in our cars and travel the miles
Do we take time in our life to just stop and smile?
Look around at the world we live in
The beauty of nature the true gift from Him
When you drive for miles through the lands here
on earth
Have you stopped and shared the things it gives
birth
Today did you stop and look at the mountains so
high
Reaching so gallantly up toward the sky
Do you see the trees and their colors so rare?

Did you take off your glasses or did you really care?

To see the colors so pure from your naked eye

Radiantly shining with their colors of dye

Did you take a moment as you rushed on your way?

One simple question: "Did you see God on this day?"

Did you hear the laughter or the sounds of loved ones so true?

Did you take time out to listen to the ones who love you?

Could you hear the water as it poured from the rain?

Did you hear the magic that fell, was it really a strain?

We hustle through life with our ears tuned out to life

Forgetting the basics that help keep out the strife

Did you hear the birds as they sang out their
songs?
Did you hear the thunder roll in its voice so
strong?
So many sounds we tune out on our way
Did you my Dear Friend? "Hear God on this
Day?"
How many times do we pass flowers on our way?
Their beautiful fragrance that could light up our
day
Smell the moisture or the rain in the air
Or the burning hot desert that scorches your hair
Do you smell the aroma of dinner cooking so fine?
Do you enjoy it, or complain time after time?
Of smells that hinder the mind and the soul
Such simple gifts in our lives, we refuse to know
The smell of the ocean as it crashes onto the shore
To the smell of the pines, do you hunger for more?
The smell of your loved ones as they gently kiss
you

Could you remember that smell if it was the last thing you do

Did you stop and smell life as you pass on your way?

Did you my Dear Friend? "Smell God on this Day,"

One of the greatest gifts of the love we've been given

Is to taste the fresh things that have been sent from heaven

To taste fresh water to help cleanse our souls

Purer than life to help us all grow

To taste the lips of your lover as they kiss you good night

Giving you comfort so you know things are all right

The taste of the sea as the air reaches your lungs

The fresh taste of nature as it caresses your tongue

Did you take time today to truly taste the things that you had

Do you remember the taste, if you didn't how sad
To taste life as you go on your way
Just one simple thing, "Did you taste God today?"
As you rushed through your day did you take time
to play?
Reaching out to loved ones as they waited today
Did you touch the love of your life as you rushed
right along?
Did you reach out to them with feelings so strong?
Did you feel the air as the wind gently blew?
Feeling its coolness, as if somehow it knew
That we are a people who seem to forget
The touch of our loved ones in life we regret
The touch of the child as it holds out its hand
The feeling of love was just part of the plan
Did you feel the rain or the sun as it warmed up
your soul?
Did you curse the weather or the bad omen the
crow?

Did you reach out to nature and look at its beauty so rare

All part of the plan that was answered with prayers

Did you feel life from the touch left astray?

Please answer me Friend? "Did you Feel God on this Day?"

Our senses were given to help us along

To help us shout out his glory in the words of our songs

So often we pass through life working and not seeing the pain

Of our Dear Loved ones that we've left out in the rain

We don't see or hear the true gifts in our lives

Our family and friends our husbands and wives

Do we see the mountains as they rise out of the seas?

Or the elegant eagles as they soar as they please

So many things we miss in our time here on earth

Do we really realize the gift of a birth?

Where children are given by the most beautiful
Hand
What greater gift for a woman and a man
The roads are full of beauty for the ones who take
care
To make time in their lives through the Lord and
their Prayers
So tonight before you kneel down to pray
Look at your Life. "Did You Know God on This
Day?"

CHEATER'S LAMENT

Why do couples in the world of today
Take vows for granted when temptation comes out
to play
Where is the truth spoken on their wedding days?
Where forever their love would be there to stay
Through the darkest of nights to the power of the
storms
Promising things to help each other stay warm
Looking into eyes, moist from the feeling
Never intending, to send their dreams reeling
Holding hands and kissing the lips of their mates
Having no doubts that God had showed them their
fate
Love so special on this day became harder than
glue
Sharing a life with the one you loved true
In these special moments no thoughts of hurting
each other exist

There's no doubt in your mind of the things you can resist
The look of a stranger as they glance fleetingly by
You don't think a thing of it with your head in the sky
Just like the planes or the balloon that rises to fast
The feelings of euphoria forever won't last
These are the times when true love wins out
Testing the bonds and the feelings that spout
For through the year's temptations comes in so many places
From the simplest gesture to the look on their faces
When you are married it's in these times that you trust
To show love and faith to you partner, to succeed or bust
What will it hurt you seem to think to yourself
Is this simple temptation worth putting your love on a shelf?

What are you thinking when you stray from the
ones you love true
Where is your mind when you search for the things
that you do
Is a kiss in the dark on a cold lonely street?
Worth throwing your life away when you try being
discreet
Lies are a burden when you try to hold them in
your soul
Wherever you go, you wonder how many may
know
It rips at your soul and your minds racked with
guilt
Your demeanor becomes torched darker than the
glaciers silt
You hide out in corners or in the back seats of cars
Wherever you can, to try to hide all the scars
For thirty years you lived a life that others tried to
live by

But for some crazy reason you give up and don't
try
To live by your vows you took thirty years ago to-
day
What were you thinking in your head on this day?
The lies came quickly and slicker than grease
So many lies you told to put your mind at ease
One thing you forgot in this crazy thing we call life
A lie will always betray you to your husband or
wife
For one lie leads to another and another on top of
that
They build up so quickly you mind races like that
of a rat
What did I say what lie did I tell her today
I need to cover my bases as I go out to play
I know what I'll do to cover my ass
I'll blame everyone else for the sins I have cast
The typical cheater tries to blame the ones left at
home

To cover their tracks to the whores where they
roam
Men are not the only ones so please remember that
fact
Women are just as guilty when they lie on their
backs
This is not a fun poem or one that we should look
shamefully away
But look at is meaning in our world of today
Vows taking between two people in front of God,
Family and Friends
According to scripture is a bond that should be
there to the end
The temptations of the world that we live in today
Is one of sinful pleasure where vows are often
thrown away?
When they are thrown out the window with ease
You destroy so many lives when you did what you
pleased

The spouse and the kids waiting for you to come home

While you were out on the streets where you chose to roam

Why don't you think of the dangers or of the gifts you may lose

While chasing after rainbows like runaway news

Why don't you stop for a second and see the looks on their faces?

How will it affect them when the lies become races?

Racing here and there to cover your tracks

Knowing if this affair breaks, you won't be able to go back

You have thrown trust and faith out the window to the ones who love you

Begging and praying for it back is just something you cannot do

For once trust has been destroyed in the heart and the soul

No matter the promises it lingers there and continues to grow

For the heart, soul and mind might try to forgive

But like the mighty elephant he remembers as long as he lives

Why marriages are thrown away on the wings of a bird

Where are those words that were so tenderly heard?

I will love you and care for you until your dying days

Honor and commitment is how my love will be played

People use drinks, drugs or affairs on stupid things

But the bottom line, it was their choice to remove their wedding rings

Spouses left behind don't be down on your self

Don't be afraid to explore you own personal wealth

You are the ones who were there for the kids

Trying so hard to keep things under the lids

The people who cheat they are not right for your soul

Be true to yourself and you somehow will know

They aren't the ones that was meant for just you

Look for the special person who will love only you.

ALASKA'S TREASURES

The eagle flies magically over the valleys so low

Through mighty mountains with peaks covered in

snow

Imagine the beauty of what it must see

To soar like an eagle what a thrill it would be

To soar through the mountains in this beautiful

land

To travel to places how amazingly grand

To see the flow of the rivers as the snow melts in

the spring

Turning the landscape into a beautiful scene

Close your eyes and imagine the things you would

see

Fly with the eagle and travel with me

To Anchorage with it streets full of life

To the mighty wilderness where it takes a will to

survive

The mountains rise out of this beautiful land

From the lowest of valleys to Denali so grand

To fly like the eagle to the top of its peak

Imagine the view of the things you could seek

You could see Alaska from the top of its world

With all of its beauty below you unfurled

To see the animals as they go on their way

The wonder of nature as it goes through its day

The moose with their calves and the bears with
their cubs

All share in the beauty of nature's club

To see the wolves in their packs as they roam

To the mighty beaver as it works on its home

The caribou migrate to the north in the spring

The majestic eagles as they spread their great
wings

The salmon in the rivers as they swim upstream to
die

Leaving their eggs to help multiply

Yes Mother Nature has blessed this great land

All part of the vision of God's mighty plan

As you travel the land to the shores of the sea
To see the great beauty and its mystery
The Polar Bears prowl in the great arctic ice
Searching for food in its quest to survive
The seals and the walrus swim and lounge in the
sun
The great whale surfaces and frolics in fun
Eskimos in their skiffs as they hunt the mighty
whale
A whole village they will feed as they raise their
sails
Dog mushers drive their dogs through the desolate
land
Gold mushers pan gold in the silt and the sand
The rivers run hard and their secrets they keep
So many lost treasures hide in their waters so deep
The mountains rise high and their summits are
steep
To the mighty glaciers with their crevices deep
Water so blue that it caresses your eye

No wonder so many live here until the days that
they die
The winter brings beauty of another kind
Such wondrous things that capture your mind
The moonlight lights up the sky with its heavenly
glow
The land is covered with a blanket of snow
The animals move in this angelic place
Searching for food in their survival race
But the beauty of winter in this land that we know
Is not in the animals or the falling white snow
Look to the skies on a night that is clear
A beautiful scene you will see up there
The northern lights dance and they'll put on a show
A vision of beauty that will be ingrained in your
soul
Colorful lights dance with a will of their own
If you stop and listen you can almost hear them
moan
To travel this land is a quest you should take

For the chance of your life for memories to make

The beauty of Alaska is so special to see

Things that have evolved throughout history

REFLECTION OF THE MIRROR

I look in the mirror I wonder whom do I see

Is the face one that I know or a complete mystery

Who is the person who lives in this place?

Is he a stranger or a familiar face?

I look at myself through the years that I've lived

What was my purpose, how much did I give?

I look at my past and the lessons I've learned

Some of them wanted but all of them earned

What did I learn from my days as a youth?

Did I learn the lessons of honor and truth?

Looking back on the times I was little and young

How many times they seemed to have stung

Those lessons I learned that sunk to the core

Ingrained in my soul for my life ever more

Always open a door for a lady you see

Respect others as much as you want to be

Show affection to the ones you love true

No matter where you roam it's just what you do

Was I a perfect child, the answer is no
Some say I was a hellion so long ago
As you grow older the things that you see
May not affect others as much as for me
The day you first learned how to drive
How great of a feeling so free and alive
The day you were married and you thought forever
more
Was just an illusion as it slammed like a door
The birth of a child and the joy that it brings
Is one of life's mysteries such a wondrous thing
The day your child walked and the joy that you felt
Those were the cards from the hand you were dealt
Seeing them grow to be young women and men
Hoping that forever they will be your best friends
For partners come and go in this thing they call life
Some stay forever while some cut like a knife
The values you believe in, were you true to the end
What is your message that you constantly send
Do you give a vibe for the whole world to see?

If you left a message what would it be?

What are your goals for the future you share?

To find someone to love and who would always be
there

Someone to share your hopes and your dreams

Where life without them is worthless it seems

We all have hopes and dreams for our futures

Will they be there if they're carefully nurtured?

We plan and we save to retire some day

Where will we be as we soar on our way?

What do we dream in this world that we live?

Do we dare dream the dream, what would we give

To live a life with the one you love true

To live out this dream, what would you do?

As for me, I think the things that I need

Are for a love to grow from the tiniest seed

One that would bloom for the upcoming years

A love so true that it would relieve all your fears

Fear of being hurt and lied to upon end

To find that special someone who would be your best friend

Does that exist in the world of today?

I believe it still does, if you can just find your way

To open your heart and expose it to the pain

The ones who love you will always remain

If they are gone or try to hurt you some way

Somewhere in time you must believe they will pay

For in the end we all will be judged by a mightier hand

The strong Word of our Lord as he sticks to his plan

Sinners will pay for the deeds they have done

No matter their paths or how far they have run

Each night that you sleep and your eyes gently close

Imagine the sweet fragrance of the elegant rose

No life is perfect as we all make mistakes

It is from this wisdom of the things that we take

Lessons learned from the pain we endured

Somehow in a new love the magic was pure

Remember no rose is perfect no matter its smell

What do you find when you look close to its shell

Some leaves are worn from the hot burning sun

Others are there waiting for life as if under the gun

When the dew hits in the early hours of the morn

A precious new rose is tenderly born

One of hope for the future we see

What will life bring is our main mystery

I think of the words that others have said

From so many people until they were dead

To live my life over, would I do it if I could?

Changing the mistakes I know some of us would

But the lessons we've learned as we passed through
our years

Somehow made us stronger through our pain and
our tears

So would I change a thing in my life if I tried?

No not at all, because my kids are my pride

See If I changed the way my life formed

Four beautiful lives would have never been born
So with the mistakes and the things I've done
wrong
My life is the way it was, and somehow made me
strong
So as I look in the mirror just what do I see
The answer is there it's just simply me.

LOVE IS LIKE WEATHER

Love is like rain with lightning and thunder

When things go bad; do we just stop and wonder

Is Love worthwhile with the one that we chose?

Is it worth chasing as the strong current flows?

When the thunder rolls do we cringe up in fear

Is it worth losing, the ones we love oh so dear?

As the thunder rolls and rattles our house

Do we scamper away and run like a mouse

When lightning strikes do we look at its flash

Do we think of our lives and how quickly they
pass?

As it flashes so bright and lights up the sky

Do we comfort our loved ones who break down
and cry?

Or is Love like a bright shining day

Where nothing goes wrong in nary a way

Does Love show up each day at our door

Full of perfection and into our hearts pour
Gifts of Love where nothing ever goes wrong
No problems to answer or to make us grow strong
Love is like the weather that's one thing that's true
Each day that you wake up you find something
new
For each day is different and new challenges
brings
To fight through together and to overcome things
Love is a battle when we're put to the test
To unite together and to give it your best
Love is a union in our hearts that we hope
No matter the weather it will never be broke
To fight through together the snow, drought, and
rain
To bond close together through both pleasure and
pain
Yes weather it changes as in each day we see
But when the going gets tough just where will we
be

Will we stand by our loved ones and help them
along
Unite together and build a fort that is strong
We think about Love and what it's about
Two souls joined together who have figured it out
That Love is the strength of our hearts and our
souls
To overcome troubles with the ones we are whole
By standing together not a problem exists
That we can't overcome and turn it into mist
So through Love and faith and the loved one you
trust
You can overcome anything and turn it to dust
For there's no greater test of a Love that is strong
As when the weather turns bad and something goes
wrong
These are the times that test our hearts and our
souls
Will we stand there beside them in the rain, sleet,
and snow?

To stay strong in Love when in struggles we're placed
Takes two special people where Love's found a place
It gives us the hope and the strength to go on
To unite together and show the world of our bond
When Love weaves it way inside of your heart
It's like a new sunrise and a new day to start
Love is the anchor that secures the boat in the storm
The warm crackling fire that in our hearts keep us warm
No matter the problems, the troubles, or strain
Love is the umbrella that protects us from the rain
Love can protect us from the troubles we see
Because Love lasts forever until eternity

GOD'S GIFT

As we think of Easter and the joy that it brings
From the past that is buried and the new days of
spring
As we reflect on the times filled with trouble and
strife
It was for these reasons, God gave His Son's life
He knew of the suffering and the pain he would
bear
This sacrifice he gave so we would know he was
there
What kind of being would put His Son through this
test
To show us He loved us and would forever be
blessed
Some look at the Bible and say, "How can that
be?"
Why would He give His Son's life, for somebody
like me

Therein lies the answer, if we look deep inside
For the Love that He gave us as He let His Son die
As Jesus lovingly looked to the people in sight
He knew all sins were forgiven as he died on that night
He didn't utter a sound as they nailed him to the cross
He'd die like a criminal, so our souls wouldn't be lost
Imagine those three men as they died on that hill
As death lingered over them and the night became still
Jesus looked toward the heavens and prayed to the Lord
Please forgive them dear God, that's what I'm dying for
The blood poured so softly as the life left His soul
What a wonderful gift was that man on the pole
Was that the end of the story where all faith would end

Was that the end of God's love that he ever would send

Did God forget the message that he let His son give

That through worship and faith through Him shall we live

On the day they removed the stone from the grave

God had taken his Son so we'd know we were saved

So where do we turn when our souls are not right

Just turn to God and His Love of that night

Love, Forgiveness, and Hope that night were given to me

God gave the life of His Son to help us all see

That the meaning of life is not mistakes of the past

But the true strength of Love that forever will last

So as we struggle with problems here on earth every day

We must reflect on the message that we learned in some way

We all are just human, that's God's special gift
But to forgive one another, our souls it will lift
As we celebrate Easter with our loved ones and
friends
Think of God's gift to us and for His love that
won't end

LIGHTHOUSE

As the mist of the ocean creeps silently in

Darkness envelopes the land like a long lost friend

The sailors at night look towards the shore

For their beacon of hope to guide them once more

For through the mist and the darkness they search
for its sign

A symbol of home, for sailors over time

For high on the cliff in a place all alone

The Lighthouse is their reassurance to help them
come home

The oceans are wild and the seas rage with a will
of their own

The protector of the depths and the spirits who
moan

The Lighthouse is there to help them when the
nights become still

Shining its light through the northern wind's chill

It stands as a fortress to those in distress

With its beacon of light to those who are blessed

The tower is as white as the new fallen snow

A constant reminder of home so they somehow
will know

Out to the oceans for the adventures they seek

There to guide them home and the treasures they
keep

A light shining bright for others to see

Where are they now as they sail on the seas?

Through the current and rocks and things hidden
below

The powerful light guides them so they somehow
will know

The safest way home to the ones they love true

Guiding them gently it's just what they do

Through the sleet and snow and the torrential rain

It's the sailors one constant in his world that re-
mains

For no matter his travels or the oceans traveled in
vain

The sight of the Lighthouse no words can explain

The lump in their throat as they see it alone on the shore

How many nights they have dreamed for it to see out their door

The Lighthouse reminds them of the things left behind

Young families and children who are there in their minds

Yes the Lighthouse gives more than light to the men of the sea

It gives them all hope of what life's meant to be

A place to call home when the winter captures the waves

A soft gentle call to help avoid the depths of its graves

For Davy Jones Locker has claimed too many lives

Tearing away the love of young husbands and wives

How many lives have been saved by its light?

When they have been lost on those cold lonely
nights
The number of young souls who owe the Light-
house their life
Giving them hope and the will to survive
Cannot be gathered by a simple counting of heads
Or the laying of flowers simply over the dead
The Lighthouse is remembered by the men and
women who know
The importance of its light as it shines its bright
glow
The hope of the seas rest on the light that shines
bright
Bringing lost sailors home safe every night

SWIMMING WITH DOLPHINS

I remember as a child how my head filled with
dreams
Of wondrous adventures and visions it seemed
I remember sitting on the beach and watching the
sea
Thinking of all of God's creatures and how they
came to be
I see the backs of the whales and the dolphin's
great fins
I wonder where they are going as they silently
swim
I close my eyes and my mind drifts away
To swim with the dolphins is what I wish on this
day
To travel through the ocean with the greatest of
ease
No burdens or trouble, just go where I please
To swim with the dolphins would be a dream come

true

What a wonderful vision, such a wonderful view
Traveling the seas to places we only dream of
From the bottom of the ocean to the waves cresting above
To swim at a pace that leaves others behind
Envisioning life in another dimension of time
As I watch them swim I see them jump for the sky
Out of the water they just seem to fly
As if jumping for glee in their world all alone
Not worrying at all for the sea is their home
How nice it would be to live the life that they live
Do they realize at all the great show that they give?
To watch them swim and the speed that they show
I would love to travel with them to the ends of the globe
To see sunken treasures in the oceans so deep
Of long lost adventures where ghosts silently creep
What do they see as they swim silently through?
What do they think of the things that we do?

Our oceans we call them as if we've bought them
As if a precious diamond or a beautiful gem
The ocean is not ours, just a gift we should treas-
ure
And of its creatures we should enjoy them with
pleasure
To swim with the dolphins in their home in the sea
To be in their world is the one wish for me
I would love to swim with them side by side
What it would mean for such a heavenly ride
To feel the waves splash gently on my face as we
go
Living my dream as the sun gently glows
To travels the depths to the oceans floor
What would I learn as I travel the shores?
We can only try to envision the thrill of the ride
Traveling with dolphins along on the tides
Alas this is a dream that I will dream for my own
As I sit here in my room alone in my home
The thrill of the dream will always keep me alive

Traveling the oceans where the dolphins survive

Yes dreams are for dreamers and for wishes to come true

To somehow do things that we don't normally do

So when you sleep at night and the moon rays are gleaming

Don't give up on the things you are constantly dreaming

For wishes come true if you believe deep in your soul

For the answers to prayers are in the dreams that you know

WE ALL SURVIVE

No matter what happens when doubt darkens your
sky
Think of the blessings that are there in your life
When the pressures of life somehow take over
your soul
And that something is wrong wherever you go
Take a step back from the things that you see
Could things be worse, and what could they be
When we are going through times filled with trou-
ble and pain
How do we deal with these tremendous strains?
Do we hold our head high and know the things that
we've done
Were the best we could do, when life wasn't too
fun
Did we look at others and judge them fairly each
day
Or judge them differently from our pain in some

way

So often in pain and hurt we seem to pass on

Our feelings so deep even though we know it is
wrong

For the older we get it seems the worse we've been
hurt

Where life didn't seem fair and we were stomped
on like dirt

Where friends and lovers who you thought would
do you no wrong

Left you alone with wounds felt too long

Do we let them win or let them think that they've
won?

By their childish games that cannot be undone

If we focus on the things they did to cause us dis-
tress

Just realize them leaving, left you totally blessed

For no one deserves people who try to hurt the
ones that you love

For that was not God's purpose when he sent his

son from above

Forgiveness is the lesson that we have learned
from his son

No matter the crimes or the things that they've
done

We must look to the future and live our lives for
each day

Looking at the blessings in the things traveling our
way

So from this day forward try to take control of
your heart

Living your life fully when the new meanings start

Look at the sunshine when you awake in the morn

Feeling its comfort as its rays keep you warm

Feel the rain hit you and the shock that it gives

Making you tingle so you know that you live

Smell the air as you've never smelled it before

Whether deep in the mountains or on a beach by
the shore

Smelling the things that will excite your brain

Leaving behind, the hurt and the pain
For as long as we breathe and we are alive
Those are the things that give us a natural high
Do we need someone to tell us we are messed up
in our heads?
They give up their lies in the things that are said
If you give into things they do to destroy your soul
It gives them the power to keep trying, because
then they will know
Stupid things taken or words said in vain
They want them to hurt you and leave you in pain
But just move on in your life as if they never exist-
ed
By showing your pride and how well you've re-
sisted
For there is no fixing people who act in such ways
Who try to destroy others until their dead in their
grave
All you can do is focus on the world around you
And center your love on the ones you love true

The light is brighter as each day comes to an end
When you know you are blessed with your family
and friends
When you are down and there seems no comfort
from the pain
Remember the people who cherish you, are the
ones who remained
There beside you through the good and the bad
Not running so freely when life became sad
For the ones who love you are always there by
your side
No matter the storm or how high the tide
For love is a commitment that should be for all
time
Not just for a moment as when the wind blows a
chime
True friends and family will be there for you
Always loving and caring you with their love that
is true.

THE GALLIANT YOUNG STALLION

The mist lingers as dawn breaks on the farm

The night gives way to dawn's gentle alarm

No sounds are heard as the sun slowly slips in

A rooster crows in the barn, as the transformation
begins

Life slowly returns to break the peaceful embrace

As the hands quickly move to prepare for the race

In the paddock the stallion moves gently, as he
watches the scene

A quiet air of confidence as if he knows what it
means

His eyes always alert as he watches the show

As the groomer preps him from his head to his toe

The muscles they twitch as if swatting a fly

As he snorts out the night air without batting an
eye

He's been here before he can sense it in his bones

It's what he's been trained for with each muscle

toned

His eyes flare with excitement as he feels it's his day

The third race in the crown as he goes on his way

He knows he's special somehow deep in his soul

What will it all mean, if he reaches his goal?

This day feels different somehow in his mind

What makes it so special, to make him one of a kind?

For races he's run and the love shows in his stride

Leaving others behind as their will slowly died

The walk from the paddock seems different today

So many new people as his eyes start to stray

He sees his trainer and jockey he has known for so long

His heart starts to react and his pulse races strong

The bridle and saddle are placed gently with care

It seems everyone's nervous as he gently stares

He feels the tension in the jockey as he mounts onto his back

As the horses start the parade on the long lonely
track
His muscles are tensing as he approaches the gate
He senses through there, his legacy waits
As he watches the others slowly load in the chute
A silence falls over him, as if everything's mute
Everything is quiet as he tenses with glee
At this chance of a lifetime, for his history
His eyes are focused as his jockey tenses in wait
As in the blink of an eye he springs from the gate
He's boxed in as he reaches the turn
As the air in his lungs bring on a familiar good
burn
He watches and waits as the others rush for the
lead
Not knowing his strength as the number one steed
He watches and waits for just the right spot
When his jockey will free him, to give his best
shot
As they round the last turn he knows it's almost his

time

To put an end to this test and sprint toward the line

His jockey releases the strain on his neck

Forward he shoots as if avoiding a wreck

The others start fading as he races by

His heart is racing as if could take off and fly

He sees the line approaching and one horse in his way

He knows in his heart he will win, that this is his day

With a burst of energy the jockey had felt times before

The brilliant young stallion took off and soared

He never looked back as he raced by the Gray

As he raced into history for his crown on this day

He somehow knew deep in his soul

The greatness it seemed for three in a row

The blanket of flowers were again placed on his back

As he stood there proudly alone on the track

He's back in the barn alone in his stall
As darkness drifts in with the day's final call
What the day meant he just didn't know
He could sense it was special as if starting to glow
As he drifted to sleep as the day came to an end
What a wonderful life he had come to transcend

WHAT IF TOMORROW NEVER CAME

What if tomorrow never came

Would we have lived today, exactly the same?

If we never opened our eyes for the break of a new

day

What would we have done differently as we went

on our way?

How would we have lived our last day on earth

Would we have realized the times we wasted since

the days of our birth?

When we awoke in the morning and wiped the

sleep from our eyes

Did we hear the sound of our loved ones as their

breaths slowly rise

Did we see the sunshine as it cascaded through the

window pane?

Or did we notice in awe the warmth that remained

Did we kiss the ones that in our hearts we adored?

Who waited so patiently for us by the door

Did we take time to smell the coffee as it gently
perked?
Did we make time in our day as we ran off to
work?
The sights and the sounds that rush by as we go
What have we missed, will we ever know?
Did we smell the roses as they blossomed today?
Or did we rush through our lives in too many ways
Did we smell the morning dew as it nestled the
ground
Did we stop to listen to Mother Nature and all of
her sounds
From the chirping of birds to the croaking of toads
Just what have we learned as we traveled our
roads?
Do we look at our lives as one endless race?
Rushing along at a fanatic hard pace
Do we stop and show love to the ones who make
up our life
Or do we rush through our days in our race to sur-

vive

Did we win the race when tomorrow never comes

Just what was the goal of the race that we'd run

Was it to see how fast we could get to our grave?

Or did we take time out for each memory to save

As we float off from our home here on earth

What did we learn since the time of our birth?

Did we hear the train whistle, or see the moon soft-
ly glow?

Did we take time to see the waterfalls as they gen-
tly flowed?

Can you remember the last thing that you took
time to see?

When was the last time, you took time for just me?

To stop and smell the flowers, or to watch children
at play

To talk to a stranger, or give someone some praise

Do we look at life through rose colored glasses?

Do we realize at all how quickly it passes?

Did we take time to see our kids as they grew up

and left home?

What are our memories of them as they left us to roam?

Can you close your eyes and smell the scent of your mate?

Would you really remember it if meant your own fate?

Our senses around us we somehow let slip by the way

Not stopping to enjoy life as we go through our days

Not seeing or feeling the gifts or joys in our lives

Ignoring the things that make us wealthy and wise

For the true worth of a man is not in the money they make

But in the joys of his life and from the gifts that he takes

For our lives were given for us to live only one time

Why did we rush through it with no reason or

rhyme

Why don't we live each day as if it's our last
Why did we rush through it so terribly fast?
We can 't change yesterday or the things that
we've done
We can't look to tomorrow in this race that we run
For if tomorrow never comes and we have lived
our last day
Did we live it our best as we went on our way
Did we show our love to the ones we love dear?
Did we live our last day with no regrets or fears?
Before we drift off to sleep when the night be-
comes still
Did we have any regrets that would destroy our
will?
Did we love one another to show our love true?
Did we share our hearts to the ones who love you?
Our time here is short and speeds by so fast
So take time each day to make a memory that lasts
Slow down your life in this race we can't win

Enjoy every second with your family and friends
Your days will be remembered not by what you've gained
But the sacred memories in the life that you framed

LIFE IN A DREAM

So many days we sit and we dream

Of beaches of sand so endless it seems

Where our worries and troubles are left back at our

door

Our spirits are calmed by the sea's gentle shore

As we look on the ocean and the grace of it all

In the scheme of the world we all seem so small

The water is clear and so calming to me

Just laying back I can be where I want to be

Closing my eyes I can be the ship on the tide

Or just cruising along on it for a ride

I can smell the ocean's salty smell as it fills up my

brain

So relaxing and soothing no troubles remain

The sun warms my body with its glowing hot rays

Releasing my energy in so many ways

The old man of the ocean seems to be calling to

me

As I sit here alone on the beach by the sea
I think of my life and the things I have done
Running a race that just couldn't be won
For the race of our life is not one we should live by
How big of a hurry are we in to die
We hustle through our lives never realizing its toll
Until one day we wake up alone and so old
Do we stop each day and realize the gifts in our
lives
The ones who struggle with us and help us survive
Or do we rush through as if on the back of a train
Not stopping at the crossings, until no life remains
Why are we rushing through life when we know?
This is our one chance to make our lives whole
For we only live once on this beautiful earth
Living and dying from the days of our birth
We look at the ocean and wonder and think
Did we really enjoy life, as we lived on its brink?
The waves rush in from the ocean so deep
Hiding the secrets and the treasure it keeps

We look for adventure in each day of our lives

Hoping for love with a gentle surprise

For the adventure of our life is in the hope that we
keep

For the beautiful gifts from the things that we reap

As I look to the ocean and the crest of its waves

So relaxing a time as I sit in a daze

Walking along on the beach for hours on end

Thinking of loved ones, family and friends

It warms my heart more than the sun's mighty
glow

I wonder somehow if they really know

That wherever I go and the adventures I seek

They are my true spirit and my soul that I keep

For what would I be if my days near the end?

Without giving my all and my love to them send

Yes as I walk along and as the moon gently shines

I realize forever these adventures were mine

Seeing kids grow into the best they could be

Feeling the warmth when they said they loved me

For no matter my travels or wherever I roam

The test of my life was right there in my home

As I awake and brush the sleep from my eyes

Where was the beach as I looked in surprise?

My kids were there gently holding my hand

Saying they loved me as if something they planned

I realize the beauty of what God gave to me

A loving family so I somehow would see

That although the world is huge and endless it seems

It means nothing at all when you wake from your dreams

The person you are isn't what others think or what they might do

But right there in your life, with the ones who love you

WHY DO WE LOVE LIKE WE DO

Why are the words "I Love You" used so haphazardly?

When we want someone to love us so faithfully

Why do some of us love so hard and so true

Living each breath for the one that loves you

Words are just words but actions are pure

To show the one that you love so they can be sure

We wonder do we know that their love is true

Why oh why? Can't they love like we do?

Some of us wear our hearts on our shirts

Hoping beyond hope that we will never be hurt

Some of us pour love out to those we adore

So why do they stomp our hearts on the floor

Why can't they love me as deep as I love?

Just where is their love when push comes to shove

How do you know when a love is so true and so deep?

That within their heart, you'll be theirs to keep

Why can't they love me back with the same fire in their eyes?

Where is the love? When will I realize?

That to love someone so true and so strong

When we put our trust in someone it goes so horribly wrong

Why can't they love the way we need them to love us

Why do all our expectations seem to end up in dust?

We trust and we hope that somehow in their hearts

The words "I Love You" are true when we are so far apart

Why do they run at the first chance they get?

When the words that they swore are so soon to forget

Why do some love until their last dying days?

While others use the words as things, to just get their way

What has happened to love that stands strong

Where within your words there a mutual bond
To love one another to death do you part
Why does it end up with sore broken hearts?
People say things like I'll forever be true
I'd never do the things, like how others hurt you
But in the blink of an eye, oh how things do
change
When within your lifetime, things are rearranged
"Out of site out of mind" it seems enters their
thoughts
Doing things that are done and shouldn't be taught
We search and we search as if lost on the sea
For someone to love us and be true as can be
Are these just lost visions of grandeur and hope?
To find someone to love you is it that remote
Love shouldn't be pain and hurt for us to endure
But one made of commitment and to be honestly
pure
So why don't we love each other the same
Why isn't it simple, can someone explain?

To find love in each other we long for in our souls

That no matter where we are for the others to know

That their love is with us in their actions and deeds

Where no reasons for doubt are cast forth by our seeds

Why don't they love me back as much as I do?

Why can't I find a love that is true?

Are we measured by the love that others give us?

What do our actions provide the ones we love and trust?

No one can define the true measure of Love

Do we somehow compare it to God's gift from above?

Are our expectations of others unfair?

Do we expect too much when they say they really care?

All we can do is in our own hearts stay true

And mean it from our souls when we say "I Love You"

PLEASE DON'T FOLLOW ME

How did I end up here, lying cold on the floor?

What has gone wrong where is my last score

My body is cold and I can't seem to respond

To the doctors and nurses as they utter their sounds

My mind is awash and confused by the scenes

Why are they trying so desperately to hook up the

machines?

What do I recall from the life that I lived?

I see everything suddenly but just what did I give

Did I give of myself for others to see?

Did I respect myself first; was I what I wanted to

be?

I can see my life as it flashes before my eyes

I can see so many loved ones that I hurt and made

cry

I see my parents and the hurt on their soul

When they realized my fate it was the drugs they

would know

How they ripped apart my youth and my dreams
All for the love of the high and the euphoria it
seems
I see my dear siblings as they look at me for their
hope
How foolish was I, instead I just ran to my dope
I could have been something in the grand scheme
of life
Why didn't I see it when I married my wife?
I turned to the drugs to help me get through my
days
Ruining my dreams as I passed through in a daze
The birth of my son should have been special for
me
But where was I, wasted on Meth and just couldn't
see
The pain on her face as she struggled alone
Praying so hard for me to finally come home
Yes the pain in their faces is so real to see
What was I thinking was it all about me?

I turned to the things that have ruined my soul

Why didn't I think, why didn't I know

The effects it would have on not only my life

But how it would affect my family, children and
wife

I feel my body convulsing going out of control

I can't figure out what's happening to my soul

The room is a blur as everything's passing by

The tube in my throat Lord I can't even say bye

I see my loved ones with worried looks of their
own

What was I thinking as I lay here all alone

Not knowing what's happening I can't feel any-
thing

The lights become bright as a giant white ring

I can't take my eyes off it as it pulls me inside

Is this what it feels like when you really die?

I drift above the room as if in a moment in time

Trying to figure out my life as if it's a rhyme

I see them tell my parents and my wife and my

child

They just shake their head as if shameful and mild

I'll never see my son throw a ball or run on the
ground

Or hear the laughter he shares and so many sounds

My wife is dressed in clothes that are tattered and
worn

Is this how I provided for the one I loved and
adorn

The drugs were the things that ripped them apart

It ruined my love, my soul, and my heart

I never saw the damage as it caused so much pain

A long lonely tale with a terrible stain

Where am I going what's happening to me

I am just twenty one, I am too young you see

I can't die like this I have so much to give

Where oh where is the life that I wanted to live

The room is dark and now there is no one there

Where did they all go why doesn't anyone care

I realize right now and that it's really too late

I have destroyed myself and sealed my own fate

I'll never feel the love again of my family and
friends

I have died all alone and for me this is the end.

WHAT HAVE THEY DONE

I wonder, I wonder what's happened to me

Where my crystal blue water I can no longer see

I feel the dark enemy flow up through my soul

Spewing out oil from the depths of a hole

Why can't they see, the damage that's been done

In their race for greed that can't be undone

My waters no longer are blue as the dear sky above

Why has this happened, where is the love

My friends that live in me are forced from their
homes

Where for millions of years their ancestors have
roamed

I look around and see all the pain that is here

My waters run deep from the flow of the tears

From my friends on the land who come to me for
their life

Raising their families, as husband and wife

Where are the kids that frolicked so free?

On the edge of my waters in the sand by the sea
Where has the beauty gone of the white sandy
beach?
Why are they so black as far as they reach?
I miss the sound of joy that it brought
As people traveled so far for the pleasure they
sought
I look through my waters as the darkness closes in
How do I tell my friends of the ocean where do I
begin
That my waters are damaged maybe beyond repair
Why did it come to this why didn't anyone care
I see the pain in their eyes as they try to stay alive
Where gills are full of sludge in their will to sur-
vive
Their scales no longer shine with the soft silver
glow
Just a black oily residue wherever they go
I see the coral dying as they can no longer breathe?
Deep in my belly in the sea underneath

The sad part of this I don't think they understand
Are they being punished as part of God's plan
All living creatures that live within me
Were all part of God's plan as part of the sea
I have given so generous to the ones who fish here
Trying my best to provide throughout all their
years
My part of the plan is to help the cycle of life
To provide abundantly and never cause strife
Now my waters are poisoned and my friends die
around me
Oh Lord! My God! What have they done, why
can't they see?
I don't hear the motors of my friends as they fish
on my seas
Why has this been done is my one woeful plea
It was the greed of a few with no alternative plan
If something went wrong to do what they can
Why didn't they know how my waters run deep?
In the depths of my waters of the precious life that

I keep

The beautiful creatures that swim within me

Can no longer live in their homes in the sea

For miles and miles of the life that I give

Have been totally shattered in the way that they
live

So tragic a problem that should never have been

For the greed of a few in their one mortal sin

I see the ones that live in me as they can swim no
more

Their oily dead bodies awash on the shore

I see the birds of the sky that live by the sea

All covered with oil as they struggle in me

If I could cry tears I would flood all the lands

For the pain in my soul I know this is not in God's
plan

To destroy my waters for the wealth of a few

And to destroy the lives of so many it's something
he would not do

I can still feel the oil gushing from deep in the hole

I see all the damage why didn't they know

My waters may never be blue again

In this race for more money they have killed all my
friends

All we can hope is to learn a lesson from the ones
who were lost

That there is no way in our world that this has been
worth the cost

LONESOME WHISTLE

Darkness settles in over the cold lonely ground

The fog rolls over the land with nary a sound

The stillness of the night imprisons your soul

The darkness releases the spirits from deep in their
holes

Leaves slowly stir in the trees without wind

As memories engulf us of our long lost friends

Memories of loved ones who have gone on before

Their spirits live in us, as they guard our soul's
door

Stars in the sky sparkle and dance as if to say

"This is our time of beauty it's not the sunshine to-
day"

The moon casts a glow over the land

With beautiful shadows and visions so grand

The silence of the night becomes unbearably
strong

Deep in your heart you wonder what could go

wrong

The dogs on the porch that have rested with ease

Ears perk to attention as if filled with disease

We stare into the night as we search for their anger

What's happened to them can they really sense danger

No other sound on this night has made itself known

The dogs never lie with their senses in tone

When out of the night a whistle blows from the front of a train

The screeching of brakes and the noises remain

All Hell's broke loose in the blink of an eye

The unmistakable sound of when someone has died

Without thinking or speaking everyone sprints from the porch

Armed with flashlights as if carrying a torch

Not knowing the cause or what they might find

They race for the tracks with one thing on their

mind

They know without uttering a word

Another soul's gone as if on the wings of a bird

People come running as fast as they can

Trying to see if it's their woman or man

The train couldn't stop at the crossing so fast

Pieces of metal were found as they raced toward
the crash

The devastation captures the mind as they arrive at
the scene

The horrible wreckage caused by this machine

The scene plays horribly from the engines bright
light

How many young lives would be lost on this
night?

The shadows twirl crazy in front of the train

As people search desperately through their fears
and their pain

An elderly woman suddenly breaks down and cries

As she grips a tender young hand as she watches it

die

A hand so familiar one she has held for so long

She remembers so clearly the nights she soothed him with song

All the neighbors have gathered and with the scream from her mind

They knew the young family they would dreadfully find

For the lady had dreamed of the visit for so many days

How she had bragged and bragged in so many ways

For in the seats of the car, a young family with dreams

Would forever be together in the heavens it seemed

Life left so quickly in the blink of an eye

A world left so sudden, as they laid there and died

The lights fade from the scene of the crash

With memories of pain that forever would last

The darkness of the night enveloped their souls

As they crossed from this lifetime, into a new one

we know

The lonesome sound of a train whistle moans

through the land

The dogs howl their death call for the woman and

man

LIFE OF A COAL MINER

The alarm clock rings, breaking the stillness of the
cold Kentucky night
With a rumbling of covers the miner pulls himself
up to turn on the light
The darkness covers the quiet valley, he knows he
will not see the sunshine today
The smell of bacon frying in the pan flows into his
brain as he starts on his way
The kids haven't stirred from their beds in this ear-
ly hour of morn
They will never hear the eerie sound of the begin-
ning shift horn
This day starts like any day in the life of the hills
A long sober journey to just pay the bills
He eats his breakfast and barely utters a word
They past the moments quietly and nothing is
heard
The thoughts are there each morning as they pass

through their routine

Will this be the last day of happiness they will re-
peat this scene?

The danger of the mines is ever present in the back
of their minds

They pray every day for the chance to leave this
place behind

He steps into each of the rooms and gently kisses
each of his angel's heads

Praying ever so deeply that saying I love you will
be not be the last words he's said

He takes his lunch box from his lovely wife's hand

He stares in her eyes, and for a moment his life is
so grand

Every morning he wipes the tears from her eyes

As she fears this will be the last time she will see
him alive

He tries to comfort her and remove all her fears

As his calloused hand gently wipes off her tears

He takes her in his arms and slowly kisses her lips

He tells her he Loves her as he departs on his trip
She will never see the moisture in his eyes as he
quickly turns to the dark
A chill runs through his body as a crow caws out
like a lark
He tries, though he can't seem to put the omen of
bad luck out of his mind
As he knows the meaning of the crow and the mys-
tery of its kind
He drives through the darkness knowing that he
must continue to go
To the black tunnel of darkness to mine the poor
man's gold
He arrives at the mine and the air seems so differ-
ent today
A feeling so different, one he has never felt in this
way
He climbs on the cart for the long lonely ride to the
face of the mine
He can't seem to shake the feeling of the crow as a

chill creeps down his spine

This day seems no different than the hundreds be-
fore

He is a miner whose father passed him the torch as
if opening a door

The seam of coal is tiny not more than four feet
high at its peak

His light shines off the ribs as in the reflections
weird shadows sneak

Today he is working on the face drilling holes for
the blast

When he is done he packs each hole with dynamite
at last

He wires the charges and stretches the wire around
the bend of the seam

"Fire in the Hole" he calls to protect his fellow
miners and those of his team

He hits the button and time seems to stand still

As the mountain rumbles from the depths of the
hills

Every man prays as they wait for the coal dust to
clear
Praying each second till the dust disappears
As soon as the blast explodes the miners are lost to
the world
Not knowing each second if they will be seeing
their own boys and girls
The families feel the earth shake miles away
And their thoughts turn to God as they pray and
they pray
Inside the mine the men all cry out for each other
Knowing things can go wrong as they look out for
another
They cry out in vain for the miner who had rose
from his bed early that morn
They search in vain for the miner as their hearts
are torn
His lovely wife feels a chill rapidly flash through
her soul
She looks to the mountain and deep in her heart

she seems to know

The miners search for the man who had shared their hopes and their dreams

Increasing their search in desperation it seemed

Out of the darkness they see a light flicker as they search and they hope

From deep in the mine comes a low moan for help as they struggle and cope

They see a hand sticking out of the pile of slate

Tears stream from their eyes as they realize his fate

He is still conscious as his life slowly fades

His thoughts turn to his family and the price he has paid

A tear slowly rolls from his eye as he thinks of the things that weren't said

How many mornings went without saying I love you as they comfort his head

The mine turns colder as the chill spreads over the land

His wife suddenly shivers as the wind seems to
carry the voice of her man
The wife realizes it's not the sound of the wind at
all
But the voice of the crow and its deathly caw
Inside the mine the life slips from his soul
Into God's hand he's transferred as it's his time to
go
The life of the miner ends all hopes and dreams
In the cold and the darkness of the lonely coal
seam
The scene will be acted out every morning in the
Kentucky coal mines
Families not knowing each day if it will be their
miner's time

The alarm clock rings, breaking the stillness of the
cold Kentucky night
With a rumbling of covers the miner pulls himself
up to turn on the light

WHAT ARE WE LOOKING FOR

What do I see when I look at myself
When so many times love's been put on a shelf
I sit and I wonder. What was the pain for?
Where did love go for the ones I adored?
As I stare at the mirror and the face that I see
What was the real truth could it really be me
Why wasn't our love strong enough to survive?
That tore us apart as a husband and wife
I stare at these walls as they close in on me
What happened dear Lord could you please help
me see?
As others walked out and left me all alone
I fear for my heart and of it turning to stone
How do I trust in people I meet?
How do I believe and somehow stand on my feet
I try to convince myself as I look to move on
Ignoring the things that are so obviously wrong
Have I become jaded by the hope of true love?

When will God show me True Love as a sign from above?

I sit by myself and think how lonely I am

Digesting the data that into my heart has been crammed

I look at my past and think lord what have I done

Fighting so hard for a win that could never be won

I realize I have given so much in this race of my life

The search for true love that would be without strife

Why do I not see the signs that are there in my face?

Things I try to ignore to help love find its place

Do I ignore the facts for pure love or how lonely I seem?

Is this the real person that I so often dream?

Is it real love or just a new race to start?

Do I think they're the one who will uplift my heart?

I see all the signs of things that are wrong

How do I convince myself and somehow stay strong

There are things in our lives that we know that are true

Whether the words are hollow or not, when someone says I Love You

Are they trying to convince us with promises and lies?

Trying to win us before our heart dies

There are things in our lives we just cannot let in

Those who lie, do drugs, or adultery we just can't let them win

A place in our hearts where they beg to become a part

To reach inside of us and convince us for a new start

Their lives of sin from their past they want us to believe

They have started fresh and turned over a new leaf

We look and we know deep down in our soul

That this is a person I really don't know

How can love be built on deceit and lies?

I realize you can't and soon it all dies

Into a grave where so many have gone

The ones who committed their love when they
knew it was wrong

I lay here in bed with the battle inside my soul

Wondering daily why I fail to accept the things
that I know

That true love is special and a bond like no other

Given from God like the love of a mother

We fail to see the times that we fall in and out of
true love

Do we realize some of these loves are not God's
gift from above?

When someone you love cannot look into your
eyes

When they avoid at all cost admitting their lies

For truth, honor, and trust are the things we must

give

To the ones of our dreams that we think we must
live

They say the eyes show the depth of your soul

They always tell the story of things we must know

People are good at promises and lies

It's the thrill of the hunt and not of a love that
won't die

For lies and deceits are such a part of their world

Where eventually "I love you" are just empty
words

We try to hold on and make ourselves believe it's a
true love that's strong

When inside our head it's screaming this thing is
wrong

Why do we throw the ones we love most under a
bus?

When we know from the first lie that this love is a
bust

We try to hold on to the barest of threads

Believing the lies in each word that is said

We see the lies and the things they hide from us each day

When we know in the long run for this we must pay

We should have standards for the ones we adore

Unconditional love is what we're striving for

We search and we search for a love that is true

The one you've dreamed of so long, that loves only you

Where inside your heart its' found a home

No matter where they go or how far they must roam

One you can trust with your entire heart

So scared in your soul they won't tear it apart

For love should be there daily wherever they go

With truth in their words and actions so all people know

They have given their soul to you without strings

To uplift your life always as they put on their ring

One thing we know lies always come back

Ripping souls apart with their brutal attack

There are no words of wisdom that I know to give
you

Make sure you're not lonely and the person has a
love that is true

In the end it's each person's choice on the actions
they do

Are we that desperate when they say "I Love you"

Make time each day to try to open your eyes

Don't be fooled by Satan with their unearthly lies

I can do this, or give you all of your dreams

Do they look in your eyes when they're talking it
seems

These are the things that I know are right there

They really don't love you and don't really care

If they rip your heart apart and stomp it while
you're down

Do they not hear your words, do they not hear your
sounds

Walk away now while you still have some pride

For you see the real person, you see all their lies

For true love is not gifts and promises that are so often broken

As careless a gift as a small subway token

Are these things we can live with as our lives wither in pain?

Will they really give in and in their lives make a change

We all know the truth, changing another when in their soul they think they are right

Building more lies with promises with no end in sight

If we believe in our Lord and somehow turn to him with our lives

He will show us the true love we must live as husband and wife

Not seeing the truth and the fact that they've lied

Destroying your will in the things that they hide

Step away from the scene or be alone with a friend

Tell them the story from beginning to end

Sometimes we realize the person was not who they claimed to be

Hiding dark secrets afraid that you'll see

The lies and deceit have caused chaos and pain

Wetting you daily as the cold drops of rain

If there is doubt in the one, you think that you love

Take heed with this warning, it may not be from above

Give it some time, but if the lies are too great

Throw in the towel or shatter the plate

We so often hear that if you love something please set it free

If it returns to your soul then it was meant to be

If they run away to another or to a faraway land

Realize deep in your heart it was just part of their plan

That through yourself and your loved ones you will surely survive

To wait on a true love, that makes you feel alive

We all deserve better is all that we hear
As we realize the truth as our eyes shed their tears
We must give up on false love with the one who
can't look you in your eyes
Ripping at your soul until the day that you die
Move on in life and true love will come along
When least expected one that will never be wrong
Don't settle in love that is one thing for sure
Never quit looking until you find a love that is
pure

JOURNEY OF LIFE

As we walk down this road of life we've been given

We wonder so often, has it prepared us for heaven

So many times we look at and crucify our lives

Carrying burdens of pain until the day that we die

Heartaches and tragedies that have transformed our hearts

Things that have changed us, we don't know where to start

To lead a life, full of forgiveness and grace

In this hectic short life, with its fatalistic hard pace

Was this what God wanted as he gave his Son's soul?

The most precious of gifts so that somehow we'd know

Our purpose here on earth has been written so long

Our journeys predestined some right and some wrong

God has a plan so often were told

Such a simple phrase, that we try so hard to hold

We question things, like the birth of a new soul

Who somehow was born, but was not truly whole

Or the death of a loved one who we thought was taken too fast

In the days of their youth and how the misery lasts

We wonder each day why things happen like this

How we wish they could return, would be our one dying wish

Our hearts linger so long on these things in our lives

The loss of our loved ones our husbands and wives

We ask ourselves daily why these things have occurred

When in our hearts it's God's gift, we so often spur

Do we look at ourselves and to the gifts that we've shared?

Do we recognize true love in the ones that have

cared?

We take things for granted in each day that we live

Not taking the moment to enjoy the gifts that He gives

So often we look at the sky without thought

Blaming the sun for the terrible droughts

Cursing the clouds and the rains that they bring

Disregarding the miracle as the flowers grow in the spring

The rainbow shows us beauty in the glory it shares

A sign from above that He shows us he still cares

Floods, disease, and disasters we question each day

Do we stop and realize that it's all part of the play

The acts in our lives that we must somehow endure

To maintain our faith and somehow be sure

No matter our lives or the things that we've done

It's between us and God in the end, to see if we've won

The battles and tests that we're given each day

True tests of our faith and how much we pray

Have we done enough each day in our hearts?

To ensure a place in Heaven when the true judg-
ment starts

I see people each day who worry in how other's
they rate

When it's the word of our Lord, who will decide
our fate

All we can do on this place that we roam

Is keep God alive in our hearts and our homes

Daily we're tested as we try to survive

By things that upset us, as we live out our lives

We must keep our faith whole and in His word we
must trust

No matter the cost, our Faith is a must

To believe in his gift as he carried the cross

So all hope here on earth would never be lost

Despite the pain and heartache in your soul

Keep his gifts close to your heart, so you'll always
know

God walks there beside you as you go on your way

Holding you gently as you live out your days

A gift in Heaven is waiting up there

Full of peace and tranquility to show that he cares

So when you are tested and think all hope is lost

Think of the gift we were given as he died on the
cross

To forgive all our sins and to help us on our way

In our journey of life to be in heaven one day

TEST OF LIFE

The journey of life is full of so many tests
Ones that haunt us until our life gives up and rests
From the birth of our children as time travels and
flies
To the death of our loved ones as they lay down
and die
Roads and bridges that we somehow will cross
Carrying our troubles and burdens, that will never
be lost
Into our lives so many troubles will creep
Wounding our souls, with scars that run deep
From the first love of your life that you prayed for-
ever would last
That shattered your dreams as if made of glass
We see so many things, that we don't understand
why
From the pain in our hearts, to the tears in our eyes
So many dreams are broken each day

Broken hearts left scattered in so many ways

The little girl standing each night at the door

Hoping and praying for her father who she will see
never more

For his life was given in a faraway land

Serving his country in the hot desert sands

The mother who looks at her children each night

Praying things will be better with tomorrow's new
light

She knows there is nothing that she would not do

To take care of them and to show her love that is
true

She would lie, cheat, or steal she realizes inside
her soul

No matter the pain she will cause, to just keep their
lives whole

Young boys look desperately to the future with
hope

Wondering if they'll mcasurc up, to the things they
must cope

So often these young boys are thrown in front of
the train
Becoming the man of the house, so totally insane
For years that should be spent in excitement of
games
Were ever so brief as young men they became
Too early to understand the meanings just yet
A life full of expectations and so many regrets
Husbands who find themselves away from their
homes
As their fears and dreams encompass their bones
The greatest of fears lives inside their hearts
As the expansion of miles that keep them apart
Why are these souls so hard on themselves?
As they place all of their dreams on top of the shelf
For in their minds they must somehow survive
To do everything, to keep their loved ones alive
From selling drugs and their bodies on the cold
lonely streets
To keep hope alive and in their homes keep some

heat

Do we judge them differently and harder than we should?

Would we exchange our lives with them, if somehow we could?

There are no answers that come to the front of our thoughts

For we all live with our own demons, ones that can't be untaught

How many times do we look upon others as they pass by our doors?

Without giving thought to their plight, and how desperately poor

These souls must be to give up their hopes and their dreams

To just care for their loved ones in desperation it seems

Too many times we look and we judge by first glance

Forming bad thoughts of them without giving a

chance

Our lives are mingled together as if in tied in a
knot

We will be judged for our actions in Heaven we're
taught

Where will be when The Gates swing open wide?

How will we be judged will they let us inside?

For our actions and words that we do here on earth

Will come back to haunt us as we are judged for
rebirth

We are our own judge as we pass through our days

The person inside us, who lives with our ways

For it is in our hearts and soul that we all must re-
alize

What we will be judged for on the day that we die

There is no right or wrong answers for the things
that we do

We are just doing our best for those we love true

Our answers will be given in the blink of an eye

As our souls pass through The Gates and to this

life say good bye

So before words of anger, actions or deeds

Think to yourself of the dangers they heed

Look in your mirror, of the life that you've had

Whether you actions or deeds will be perceived as
bad

Your own consciousness will somehow shine on
your soul

To look yourself in the eye, you will definitely
know

Whether your life here on earth has been the best it
could be

For in these deeds will be decided, where you
spend eternity.

EVENING SHOWERS

As I close my eyes and think back to my past
Of things I remember of how our days were cast
Sitting on the front porch feeling the sweltering
heat
A place where all neighbors happen to meet
You could sense the storm brewing way before it
began
Just like an hour glass full of fine sand
The breeze gently stirs and into your bones send a
chill
An eerie silence seem to creep over the hills
As the clouds race above and darken into a devil-
ish glow
You could smell the storm brewing well before it
would show
The musty smell of the earth somehow reached in-
to your soul
Giving you wisdom of God's power and how it

takes its toll

The lightning flashes out like a wondrous spear

You count one, two …then BOOM the thunder
rolls as you cover your ears

The sweltering day of summer has changed in a
flash

As the earth changes its face as if removing its
mask

As you look to the mountains you see the rain
coming in sheets

And the sound of it coming sounds like millions of
feet

The earth's face changes in the blink of an eye

As the steam rolls off the ground and the creatures
they fly

As you sit on the porch and watch this mystical
show

It's one of God's miracles that we have all come to
know

As we sit and we watch water pour off the roof of

the house

The world becomes quiet as silent as a mouse

You hear the drum of the rain beating off of the ground

No one utters a word as if afraid to make the faintest of sounds

The show captures our minds as we are slowly pulled into it

The spectacle of nature as if written in scrip

The storm passes quickly and leaves us in a daze

The storm clouds disappear and the sun takes their place

But the show is not over as we look to the skies

God hasn't forgot to give us another special surprise

An arch of such beauty that shines through the air

A colorful rainbow, so we will know he is there

They say at the end of each rainbow is a full pot of gold

But the beauty of each rainbow is in His Love we

are told

That he is with us each day as we press on our way

That through the darkest of times he is there in our
day

No matter the storm or the troubles we see

That if we believe in his Love that our souls will
be eased

When your day is the darkest and you feel all hope
is lost

Look to the Heavens, His Love, and its cost

A rainbow of beauty he gave for our sins we are
told

The life of his son as His Rainbow with its own
pot of Gold

AURORA BOREALIS

The miles I've traveled over the years

To be with my loved ones, I loved so dear

The roads were endless, as I've driven so long

Where the wind howls and moans a lonely sad
song

The darkness spreads so far through the land

Like a tight fitting glove that covers the hand

The cold bites bitterly through my bones with a
chill

The animals stalk their prey, with an iron clad will

Snow whips off the mountains and spreads through
the valley so low

Giving the cold winter night an eerie white glow

The cold seeps it way to the depths of your bones

Oh so many miles and so far from home

The sound of the wheels as they crunch over the
road

Time seems to stand still as if locked in the cold

The beauty of the night although so eerie it seems
Such beauty it shows as if out of a dream
The shapes of the mountains loom as if giants they
stand
Guiding you through the maze of this beautiful
land
They stand as guardians to those who enter in
peace
For the beautiful image, will leave them at ease
The lights bounce across the skies with colors so
rare
There's not much to do, but just stop and stare
Aurora Borealis is what they are called
Northern Lights to the novice as they stand there in
awe
Lights flashing across the sky in a pattern so rare
Dancing their dance as if nary a care
Lights flicker and jump from one place to another
Such beauty of life, from God's gift, the earth's
mother

If you listen you can hear the night crackle in sound
The whispering moan, as the lights dance around
Colors so different it's hard to explain
A shower of lights as if caught in the rain
A prism so wonderful as the lights softly flow
Over the landscape in this land that we know
For the guardians of lights in the mountains stand tall
As if searching for love or a new star to fall
Lights searching for loved ones throughout the years
So many young souls that were frozen in fear
The lights search for answers, as these souls are part of their team
Where many have died as they laid there and dreamed
Their souls seem to ride on the crest of these waves
Searching so desperate for the way back to their

caves

The bears, the raven, and moose that roam free

All part of the magic we've come to see

This land is magical a mystery at best

To travel throughout, we know we've been blessed

So many have traveled from countries afar

To see things taken for granted, right in our back
yard

Is it magic or a much bigger show

Such a great mystery, we'll just never know

These lights bring lessons of the land that we love

Where so many questions are answered, from the
Glory above

For in their beauty and dance that they bring

Warms the depths of your soul what a wondrous
thing

Once your heart's seen the mystery of lights

They will travel with you on the cold lonely nights

For the magic of the lights will live in your soul

For the length of your life, you'll always know

The lights will remain, far after you've gone

But you will be with them as they sing out their

song

That is the magic of the lights of this great land

They pull you in gently and take hold of your hand

They will travel with you wherever you go

Inside your heart, deep in your soul

ANGELS OF MERCY

The clock ticks softly as the new shift begins
How many lives will be saved by the end?
The gowns are white as pure as their souls
These special young people to work they go
They prep and they scrub not knowing what for
What will be the next crisis that slams through the
door?
A sterile room awaits them for their duty today
To help save the lives of those who have strayed
Into danger or for hearts that have quit
For those who stare into heaven as their light's
dimly lit
These angels of mercy are there through good and
the bad
Wiping away tears of happiness as well as the sad
A special soul it takes to do the work of these few
Not many could do, the work that they do
So many emotions each day they endure

From the birth of a baby to the call of death's door

What kind of person can put each day on the line?

Praying to Heaven for the strength to define

The balance of life so delicately drawn

How just the slightest mistake can go terribly
wrong

The comfort they give to a child who's hurt

From the tiniest scratch as they fell in the dirt

To loving support they give to the family and
friends

Of the poor lonely soul, whose life is starting to
end?

Soft gentle hands that soothe the sweat of disease

Somehow brings comfort to souls filled with un-
ease

They wear their hearts on top of their smock

Where it's inside their chest its solid as a rock

The pain that they see each day in their life

They must hide it somehow from their husbands
and wives

From lives hanging by the barest of threads
To keep it in balance inside their heads
They walk the halls tending to those in pain
Keeping the love for their families is their constant
strain
They hold onto souls that can leave in the blink of
an eye
Encouraging the fight so the souls will not die
Such a terrible strain for these soft tender souls
Do we really thank them as they make our lives
whole?
For in our grief of the moment we tend to bypass
These beautiful people who make our lives last
Nurses who tend to us through the scariest times
Who nurse us to health and rekindle our minds
If you've never noticed these soft gentle souls
As they desperately work just so we know
That a caring young person is working for you
So you can return to your family who loves you so
true

For it's in this love that God really shows
It's through these "Angels of Mercy" that He lets
His love glow
They carry the spirit of life as it weighs on their
hearts
To start each day anew is an honorable start
We tend to see things so simple and plain
But often ignore the ones, who cure us of pain
At the end of the day, the smocks that were so an-
gelic white
Are covered with blood for those they helped fight
Yes, heroes come in different shapes and sizes
With hearts full of gold so full of surprises
These Angels of Mercy deserve our love of tonight
So when they lay down for sleep their souls will be
light
Free of all worries and feelings of doom
To know in their hearts that God's love's found a
room
For these are the souls we should pray for each day

To find peace in their hearts in some sort of way

DO THEY SEE ME?

As I lay here each day watching the days pass
through the seasons
Wondering if my Lord has spared me for some
reason
I see the birds chirp as they fly fleetingly by
Through the warm days of spring to the dark win-
ter skies
People rush by in their life every day
What thoughts enter their heads as they go on their
way?
As I lay here in bed wracked with this disease
Oh what I would give to go as I please
But my Lord has a purpose for us we are told
One we must burden and somehow be bold
I have no idea why my arms and legs won't react
anymore
For the simplest task, or just go to a store
I know there is a purpose and a plan just for me

But throughout my days I wonder if anyone sees

I wonder do they see me for who I used to be

A person who could run and skin both my knees

I lay here each day and watch people walk by my door

Wondering what thoughts they are thinking, how dreadfully poor

Do they see my eyes twinkle at their voice as they say?

How are you doing my dear? Are you having a good day?

Do they see the tears fill my eyes for the time that they share?

Just the smallest of gestures to show that they care

My body is useless it doesn't function at all

But inside this body is the spirit of the ball

Yes I wonder if they see the twinkle of my eye

Or the days that are bad where I can't help but cry

Yes the nurses and doctors they come and they go

Trying their best to help ease my soul

My mind and my voice are still vital and strong

It gives me the strength to somehow sing out my song

One of joy that can't be broken by this body I'm in

As I go through each day trying to lift up my chin

Yes I wonder if people see the person who lives inside me

One who cares for others, can they really see

How can they see if they don't take time each day?

To think of others as they go on their way

Do they see the pain in others as they pass them on the streets?

Do they take time to know the people they meet?

So many days we pass others in pain

Where just simple actions can help them with their strain

For love of each other is something we take for granted?

When so often our world is so terribly slanted

So often I wonder as I lay here in bed

Why do we rush through our lives until we are dead?

Why don't we take time for the ones left without?

Why don't we take time to help others out?

Just a simple touch on the cheek can change someone's day

Making them smile as they go on their way

Why can't people see how the simplest task

Can help mark their legacy and a memory that lasts

So as I lay here I don't wonder what the Lord had in mind

I know there is a reason for my Lord who is kind

If through this life I touch someone's soul

I will know in my lifetime that it made my life whole

So do they see me as I lay here each day?

I know that they must for my Lord shows me each day

From the gentle smile that crosses their lips

These small simple pleasures they make my heart
flip
My one hope in life that I would hope for my
friends
Take time out of your day to touch someone by the
end
For the simplest task means more than you'll know
In the darkest of nights you can touch someone's
soul
God is my guide as I live through each day
Just trust in his mercy as you go on your way
He will show you the light to help touch some-
one's life
To help them with their burdens, their trouble and
strife
So do you really see me as I lay here, with no
movement at all?
Just remember one day I will be the center of the
ball
When my lord calls me, my soul will rise high

As I dance through the heavens and fly through the skies
As you see me here, this body will never burden my soul
My spirit will be in heaven and dance so you know
Our time here on earth is ever so short
Just a passing of time through this life as a port
Our souls will be remembered for what we have done here on earth
Being judged for our actions, until our rebirth
Do unto others as they would do unto you
But remember to show love to those that love you
\

STRESS

There comes a day inside your head
Stress takes over and you wish you were dead
Stress the silent killer we're so often told
Where in the heart killed the ones who were bold
Stress comes in various strains
No one sees completely its terrible pain
A man going to school after forty long years
Because the loss of a job was costly and dear
Retraining his mind and the pressure it brings
The stress takes its toll what an enormous thing
The mother who tries to feed her baby each day
With no source of income Lord how will she pay
Tears fill her eyes for the things she must do
To provide for her family and the ones she loves
true
Lie, cheat, steal, or sell herself on the street
Working all day and dead on her feet
A child who pours over his homework each night

Praying to heaven he is doing it right

For stress of his grades is such a battle to him

He knows when they are bad the beatings begin

A drunken father who never made it in his life

Forces stress on his family his children and wife

Try to be perfect is the best they can do

No one in their right mind should have to live like they do

No matter the job or the role in our life

Stress is a constant that seems to cut like a knife

What are our first thoughts when we wake up each day?

Lord why do I have so many things that I must do today

The knot in our stomach seems to grow twice as fast

Causing anxiety that you just can't seem to get past

It tortures your head and it splits it into

Lord how can I endure this it's all up to you

Is one stress stronger or weaker to me?

There is no answer stress is all that I see

Muscles tighten in your neck and your back

Convulsions surround you, when the pain is intact

How do we deal with this thing we call stress

How in our lives do we take time to rest?

Why isn't it done, what are you waiting for

Constant complaints that pound on our door

Its seems there should be an easy answer to make
our life complete

But at the end of the day we feel exhausted and
weak

Do I have an answer to help guide you along?

The answer is no, when stress is too strong

I think of a friend who gave up all that she had

The stress had destroyed her will, how terribly sad

By giving up things that she knew she could live
without

That my friends is someone who truly figured it
out

You only live once in this circle of life

Try to take time in each day to live without strife

Blank your mind and take several deep breaths

Then open your eyes and see life at its best

Take a walk with your family and hold each of
their hands

No pressure or stress just being part of the clan

Put work aside at the end of each day

Don't bring it inside there's a much better way

For our children are young only once in their life

Spend time with them and your husband or wife

For love comes back four fold we are told

But death will come quicker if you give up and
fold.

THE OLD MAN

The old man shuffles to the mirror to start off his day

What once were his blue eyes now have turned gray

He stares at the mirror and can sense a change is in store

Something so strange, yet he can decipher no more

Time has passed over him as he went through the years

As all the memories are there so perfectly clear

A smile crosses his lips and he thinks back to his youth

Where a handshake was solemn and your word was the truth

His thoughts of a young boy who was chasing his dreams

Trying so desperately to please others it seemed

For what was his dream from the days he was young

Just a small wild kid who some say was high strung

Where will you be? What will you become?

A success to a few and a failure to some

As he grew older he remembers with ease

Of nights on the town to do as he pleased

A grin lights up his face as he remembers the kiss

The first one of its kind, one he would remember and miss

For the girl of his dreams and the first kiss of his life

Was from his dear lady who would become his wife

He can feel the tenderness as if she had just brushed his lips

Those special moments that would make his heart flip

They would grow old together until the Lord called her in late May

From deep in her sleep, God called her to Heaven one day

Oh how he missed her love so strong

The one who loved him and consoled him with her bond

His thoughts drift to his children the ones they had lived for

They may not have been rich, well in fact they were poor

But love held them together when things didn't seem right

Huddle together in the cold late at night

He remembers the games as he watched them play with their teams

Trying so hard to fulfill all their dreams

They have all moved away as he was left all alone

Just him and the walls that make up his home

Pictures adorn the walls of the house

No other sounds it's quiet as a mouse

Where did the laughter go crosses his mind

What happen to it? Did it vanish in time?

Years that he spent working hard all his life

Trying so hard to provide for his children and wife

What happened to the young vibrant man?

Who was first in the line to fight for his country and land

The old uniform hangs in the closet with care

Just a reminder of friends lost in wars that weren't there

For sometimes in battles they were taught that it was really not war

Just a battle of numbers where politicians kept score

He steps back from the mirror and feels different inside

All of his memories have filled him full of pride

His old back is hunched over he doesn't stand tall anymore

His body's been tortured and tremendously sore

He looks out the window and the sun has risen deep in the sky

He takes in its warmth as he tenderly sighs

The wind is blowing in the trees a soft gentle sound

A whisper at most but in his ears it seems to pound

Where are you at it seems to beckon so clear

Why are his eyes watering with the warm salty tears?

He turns to his closet and he takes down his Sunday's best

Why does he feel today like he needs to sit down and rest?

He combs his hair and shaves the gray hair off his face

His sits down in chair yet his heart doesn't race

He stares at the walls and holds a faded picture in hand

One of a family with his wife and her man

He stares at the photo while a tear fills his eye

He smiles once then he drifts offs and dies

EMBERS OF LIFE.....

As light flickers off the dying embers from the
flame of a fire

Does the same happen to our hearts when we lose
our desire?

Our desire to make life better for the ones we love
dear

Do the ashes char our hearts and leave us full of
fear

What is the reason for this transformation of what
we've become?

From two people in Love who are two souls not as
one

What would it take to reunite what has been lost

What's the price for true love or how high's the
cost?

When wedding vows are said they should always
remain

True in our hearts and there stay the same

Lies and deceit were never part of the vows

Their vicious intent to destroy us somehow

Can people overcome issues of trusting their mates?

Will opening their hearts destroy both their fates?

How do we live in a world without trust?

When within the love of your life it's faith that's a must

A world without trust creates anger and rage

It encloses your heart as if you're trapped in a cage

What do you do when mistrust leaves you alone?

Do you walk away from the ember until finally it's gone?

Is the love of your life worth walking away?

To walk from the ember until it's dead in its grave

Or will you fan the ember to life with a will to survive

A total devotion to bring the flame back to life

So many in the world choose to let the ember just die

To just walk away and to not even try

There are a few souls that no matter the cost

Will keep fanning the flame until all hope is lost

But just fanning the flame will not keep the fire alive

It's the will of the people to live their lives without lies

It's putting their trust, their faith and their dreams

Into the hands of another, what a huge chance it seems

What a risk to take with your heart and your soul

To trust in someone and to let yourself go

As we look at ourselves and the gifts in our life

What price would we pay for our flame to survive?

There's only one answer to the questions that be

Is to look in the mirror and see whom do we see

Is the face that we see, a face without sin?

Or a face of someone who doesn't know how to begin

To change from the way that we have lived in the past

By changing our life into a new molded cast

So when you look in the mirror, don't take a quick glance

Focus on the fact this might be your last chance

For our time here on earth is all together to short

Where will we be when they read our report?

I know I have failed miserably in this report card of life

There have been too many people I've hurt and told lies

Will my final report be a failed grade at best?

164

As I look in my mirror, I know I failed all these tests

I can't expect someone else to revive my flame

For it to die into an ember there's no one to blame

The fault is mine, as I look at the mirror

My eyes tell the story of the ones I've hurt here

Is it too late to rekindle my fire?

To start living my life with a new zest and desire

It's never too late until your foots in the grave

To change direction in life and that ember to save

There is too much trouble and pain in our world here today

For me to contribute to it makes me feel worthless some way

There is only one person who can change you again

It's the person from the mirror, who knows you from within

Are we the person we've wanted to be all our lives

Or have we failed miserably, does our face really lie

The embers of people around the world are still there

To rebuild the flames it just takes someone to care

Care for yourself and for those you love true

Be true to yourself and they'll be true to you

The best we can hope for in this life that we live

Is to keep our flame burning and from its warmth we give

To others around us the true meaning of love

As we remember each day God's gift from above

Cherish yourself and live a life that is right

You'll be constantly blessed as you lay down at night

So the next ember you see, reflect on its meaning

Our lives are for real and were really not dreaming

FUTURE

We hear tomorrow will be a much brighter day

But where is tomorrow and where does it stay

The future we see is not very clear

What will it bring to the ones we love dear?

The future seems murky with dark cloudy skies

Why wait till tomorrow to fulfill our lives

Our futures are shadows that hide in our dreams

The future is puzzlingly to us though it seems

We wait for tomorrow to do things from today

Not realizing at all if we'll be there to say

The words "I Love You" to the ones in our hearts

If we weren't here tomorrow would it rip them apart?

We take things for granted in each day of our lives

We often lose focus on our friends, family, husbands and wives

For words left unspoken can't be pried from your lips

If tomorrow finds you in death's somber grip

So not doing or saying the things that you feel

Could in all reality your legacy seal

Do you want to be remembered as someone who cares?

Or be thought of as someone who wasn't actually there

Our lives are all fickle a mystery at best

So why are our lives constantly put to the test

A test of devotion, faith, truth, and our Love

It seems a constant challenge from the Good Lord above

But it's not that, I think we realize

God's Love is there to always be prized

So where does it come from, what don't we know

That the challenge of life is the future we sow

For the past we can't change and the present is now

So we must look to the future and change it some-
how

To learn from our past and mistakes make no more

To look toward the future and it's bright shining
door

We all have demons behind us and it's our choice
to make

To let them torment us daily or from them let us
break

For the future can be bright if we give it a chance

By not looking backwards and today take a stance

To stand firm and strong to the things we've done
wrong

Commit to ourselves to not bring them along

Into our future where they can cause so much pain

Within each of our hearts and turn sunshine to rain

For the future is full of visions of hope

And the basis for that is a much wider scope

So will the future be better no one truly knows

We have to trust in ourselves, and the way our heart flows

So what have we learned in this life that we've known

There is no certain future that's written in stone

What do we do when our souls are racked with un-ease?

We try to show love, to those we must please

For to give hope and comfort to their heart and soul

That our love will go with them wherever they go

But what if tomorrow the sun doesn't rise

Would our last words be remembered as Loved or Despised?

The future is something that none of us knows

And the past in our hearts we must let it go

For today is the reality we know without doubt

If we don't show our love daily, we haven't figured it out

We should show those we love dearly that their lives are worthwhile

And by just being there, in our heart brings a smile

We should live for today the answer is clear

To share our hearts and our souls with the ones we love dear

For the future you see might never brighten our door

And our words left unspoken will be buried for sure

So show love today to someone special and true

By just a simple expression in the words "I Love You".

MARRIAGE

Why is marriage in the world of today?

A thing taken for granted and just tossed away

Why do so many crumble because of some rifts

When we know in our heart of God's special gift

His power of Love and his forgiveness so bright

Was proven the day Adam and Eve took their first bite

God's Love and compassion in our heart it resides

To overcome problems we must stand side by side

We must look at the world of today that we live

The gift of Love to each other, every day we must give

To stand by your partner that you have loved oh so long

To hold them so gently and to show them you're strong

For trials and tribulations, we all must endure

To overcome them it takes a Love that is pure

Each day is a struggle that we deal with in life

For marriage is a journey for every husband and wife

An unknown journey that starts each day anew

To be traveled so carefully with the ones that Love you

For every new day brings danger and fear

We must show our Love daily to the ones we love dear

For it's human nature to have fears and deep thoughts

But through small acts of kindness to relieve them were taught

Words of affection, small hugs, or a soft gentle kiss

Is the foundation of marriage that we so often miss

Our lives are jumbled as we live them each day

We pass through so quickly even to our dismay

So when we lay down to sleep in our beds every night

Did we do anything to make our loved one's life bright?

Some small act of compassion that might seem so remiss

But to your dear loved one, it was certainly not missed

As we travel each day, as we pass out the door

Did we take time to say "I Love You", or to show something more?

As we look at our lives, as we hurry and rush

It seems it's no wonder marriages turn into mush

So what can we do to survive marriage today?

Make time each day to show your love in some way

God's gift of marriage is his gift from above

Something to be cherished and constantly loved

We all make mistakes that cause others great pain

We turn skies of sunshine into great sheets of rain

What do we do when our lives fill up with stress?

Do we just run away or do we stand up to the test

Do we unite together and stand side by side

Or do we abandon our loved ones and run off and hide

Marriage is a sanctuary and full of God's grace

To the one you vowed forever to inside your heart keep a place

I look to our ancestors and to the struggles they bore

Marriage and love was the rock, for the ones they adored

I look at the history of their trials each day

No matter the trouble their love showed them a way

Divorce wasn't an option and was seldom heard

Because before God above they had both given their word

They would love one another to their last dying breath

To Love and to honor until at last there was death

So what have we learned from the ones of our past

That marriage is sacred and a bond that should last

Don't throw it away as if it means nothing more

Then something bought cheaply at a local dime store

So work at your marriage a little each day

Because to your dear children, you both light the way

A light that will guide them as the ones that we've seen

That marriage is special and can become quite a dream

Remember mistakes from the past, you can do nothing for them

But the future is God's blessing, a gift given by Him

Don't dwell on the past or mistakes that were done

Live for each day and with your spouse have some fun

Work out your problems and you'll soon realize

That God's gift of Love was when he let his Son die

His ultimate gift that was given that day

Was a pure gift of Love, to show us the way

Don't ever give up and in the dear Lord we trust

Our husbands and wives are God's gift to us

POSITIVE THOUGHTS

As I sit here tonight thinking of you

The one who I love so devotedly true

What are the thoughts that cross my mind?

Are they the right ones, the ones that are kind?

I have looked at myself for days in the mirror

Searching my soul for things to be clearer

What is the best way to live the days of your life?

What should you do to uplift your wife?

Positive thoughts are the answer it seems

Reaching into your heart and releasing your dreams

For positive thoughts can make the difference in you

And shower more love on the ones you love true

Too many years I have struggled in pain

Fighting negative thoughts were my constant strain

Have I waited too long to truly figure it out

What are the best thoughts is what it's all about

Do you want the one you love to be hurt by uncaring words?

Or praised from the highest with the words that are heard

I have made a mess out of chasing the wrong things

Using negative thoughts and the words how they sting

I have made a choice for myself and the ones I love true

To live my life fully in all the things that I do

To use positive thoughts for the rest of my days

To showered them with praise as I go on my way

For thoughts can be mental and leave others dis-
tressed

When in their hearts all they want is to be blessed

We make our own choices in life as we go

Do we think of others do they really know

Those words of destruction leave a graveyard be-
hind

Things that hurt them and clutters the mind

So what can we do as we travel each day?

Think of positive thoughts as we go on our way

I have searched in my soul and the answers are
plain

The use of positive thoughts will keep us from go-
ing insane

So to my true love no more harsh words will ever be said

Until the day that I die and they lay me down dead

For she deserves words that uplift her soul

Words of praise so that she always will know

She is my world, my lover and friend

The one I hold dearly until eternities end

www.ingramcontent.com/pod-product-compliance
Lightning Source LLC
Chambersburg PA
CBHW070957040426
42443CB00007B/552